# $\mathcal{A}$ Recipe *for* Dreaming

# $\mathcal{A}$ Recipe *for* Dreaming

# BRYCE COURTENAY

ILLUSTRATIONS BY *Anie Williams*

VIKING
*an imprint of*
PENGUIN BOOKS

# Introduction

*T*he greatest inheritance we humans have is the gift of speech. The gift of words is also the gift of imagination. With imagination anything is possible and we all potentially have a much larger share of this gift than ever we use. That is, if we choose to work at it. The paradox is that in the process of gaining knowledge, very little time is given over to stimulating our imagination to use the knowledge we've gained to dream new pathways and new outcomes.

We are told at an early age to stop dreaming and to start concentrating; whereas, in fact, one of the most important processes of gaining knowledge is learning how to dream, to add imagination, to learn to concentrate on possibilities so as to extend the sum of what we already know. Not only 'What is?', but also, 'What if?' Any new thought requires greater concentration, more intellectual energy to bring into effect, than one that has been recycled.

'Don't' is a word children hear far more often than 'Do'. 'Think before you jump' is a caution we are routinely taught during childhood. Humans are instinctively afraid of the unknown and the untried. We love the safety of numbers; we hate risk; we strive to be stereotypical and unremarkable. We often use terms of disparagement for people who think outside the square or don't fit into our preconceived notions of how to behave.

Orthodoxy, the notion of being like everyone else, isn't necessarily a bad thing. All effective societies depend to a large degree on compliance and precedence. Too many of our leaders are intellectual street-sweepers – they keep the place nice and tidy, maintain the status quo and the conventional wisdom, but add nothing to the intellectual and spiritual sum of who we are, what we need and where we're headed as a society.

It is the dreamers who are the true leaders. Without them we would still be living in caves, albeit very tidy ones. Trying something new and different always carries a margin of error. Initial failure is the precursor to success. In other words, we learn from our mistakes and nothing is more certain than that we will make mistakes. Mistakes, errors of commission, are the bricks that build the structures required for successful outcomes.

If we don't take our imaginations beyond the norm, we deny the greatest gift we humans have been given. Putting our imaginations into action to find new ways to go is synonymous with the act of dreaming. It is essential to inwardly visualise the destination, to clearly see the dream. To become a dreamer you need only to ask permission from yourself. Remember, whatever the dream, no matter how daring or grand, somebody will eventually achieve it. It might as well be you.

*Grabbing the moment*

Birth

*tic — toc — tic — toc — tic — toc —*

Death

## *Cloud drift*

Can you remember when you were a kid
and you'd lie in the grass on your back and
watch the clouds scud above you and dream of what
you were going to be when you grew up?

Well, what happened?

# *A recipe to dream*

Take one dream. Dream it in detail.

Put it into your own hands. See its final outcome

clearly in your mind. Mix it with a little effort and

add a generous portion of self-discipline.

Flavour it with a wholesome pinch of ambition.
Stir briskly with confidence until the mixture
becomes clear, the doubt separated from the resolution.
Bake at an even temperature in a moderate oven
until the dream rises and is firm to the touch.
Decorate with individuality. Cut into generous
portions and serve with justifiable pride.

Approached in this manner, life is a piece of cake.

Good luck

Good luck is what always comes to those who use the
recipe for dreaming and having dreamed their dream, never,
never give up until they have achieved it.

# Dare your genius to walk the wildest unknown way

Go where you've never been before.
Dream up a destination, a path to follow, the wildest
unknown way, over rocks and scrag, across high hills
where the winds bite cold with malice, through deep
mysterious valleys where the wild things roar and echo
and rumble and stamp and hiss great clouds of steam
from their terrible huffing ways.

Dream the impossible dream and
start walking towards it.

On the way you'll quite
soon learn what it feels like
to be beaten up, chewed, spat
out, mauled, ripped apart and
given up for lost.

This is called 'experience'
and it's very, very valuable in
life, because what you mostly
learn from it is that you were
more afraid of what *might*
happen than what *did* happen.
Most successful outcomes are
achieved by calling a series
of conventional bluffs.

## When the strange becomes familiar

One bright, sunny morning
you'll discover that the wild and
unknown way you took is carpeted
with moss and strewn with tiny flowers.
It has become a familiar path, a well-trodden
direction that has put you miles ahead of anyone else
and much, much closer to achieving
your once-impossible dream.

# The value-added you

There's you, good old you, not too bad,
not too good, safe, sure, reliable,
steady as you go. You.

A bit of a deterioration really from the perfect baby your
mother claims you were. What can you possibly add to the
sum of yourself that would make you love yourself more?
Not something for the kids, or your husband or wife,
or your friends. No more self-sacrifice or feeling sorry for
yourself. Add something that makes you more valuable
and lovable to the person you talk to all the time.

Keep thinking for as long as it takes to find the value you want to add. Unless you're perfect already, it's generally not too hard to find at least one 'If only...' You know, if only I had the time, money, education, intelligence, talent, I would...

If you're going to add value to yourself you must make yourself the top priority. You are, after all, the most urgent project you can possibly undertake. Working on yourself is the single most rewarding thing you can do.

Eventually someone will benefit hugely from the result.

*She gave me a look of
white-hot apathy...*

'It's okay for you,' she said, looking down at
her hands resting in her lap. 'You're clever. I can't
tap-dance, I can't dare my genius, I can't find
any unknown paths to walk, I can't even think
of anything to dream about. I get so bored thinking
about myself, the hands at the end of my arms rock
me into a stupor. My mind is manure.'

She paused and looked directly up at me.
'Quite frankly, Bryce, all of this hopeful crap you go
on about makes me want to throw up in your lap!'

## *First thing tomorrow*

Find a comfortable chair, close your eyes,
put your hands in your lap and start
learning how to dream again.
Dream about what you've already been.
Repeat this the next day and the next.

After some ten days you'll get the
knack of dreaming again. You'll begin
to regain the long lost art of dreaming.
Dream what has yet to be done.
Dream a direction for yourself.

## *You were not born empty*

God formed you with perfect feet and hands
and a heart that beats non-stop, sometimes
for a hundred years. He made you complete.
Why then do you assume He made you empty?

He didn't, of course. You inherited a thousand
generations of wisdom, skill, poetry, song, all the

sunrises and sunsets of knowledge past. You are the sum of all the people who went before you.

You are a refinery of inherited intellectual wealth. The full flood of antecedent wisdom is piped and stored within you — how to climb the highest mountain, slay the biggest monster, how to survive fear, and how to summon your own courage and take pride in your wonderful intelligence. Inside you are more possibilities than you can possibly use up in one lifetime.

If you can dream it, you can do it, because the instinctive knowledge of how to succeed is already programmed within you, waiting to be turned on. Waiting to flow like a river as you come on stream.

# *If you don't know where you're going then how will you get there?*

Visualise! Make pictures in
your mind. See the destination.
Imagine your arrival.
Dream in perfect detail.
See yourself the way you want
to be when you arrive.
See yourself arriving. Make yourself
a road map and study it every
day until you know the
destination by heart.

*The helping hands*
*you're going to need in life*
*are located at the end*
*of your arms*

Put yourself into your own hands.
Everybody has two. You can use them
to get a hand-out, sit on them and do nothing, or you
can use them to get a serious grip on yourself.

But when you've put yourself in your own good
hands, don't forget to give yourself
an occasional pat on the back.

Say, 'Well done, pussycat, you're doing okay!'

## *Get away from the bottom and the top will take care of itself*

It isn't hard at the top. It's easy.

It isn't crowded and it's really quite civilised.

What's hard is the bottom – down there you'll find

one hundred times more competition. Down there

is where people stand on your teeth so they

can get a firmer foothold on the first rung

of the ladder out of hell.


Why then is it that most people seem

to be so afraid of success that they'll do

almost anything to avoid it?

## *When you're skating on thin ice you might as well tap-dance*

Stick your neck out, volunteer, have a go, reach out beyond your best performance and when you do, do so with style, élan, panache. You will learn more from a brilliantly executed failure than from a success planned within the dreary safety of what you already know.

Winning easy is boring, pointless work.

## *Walking down the centre of the road*

You've spent your life walking down the
centre of the road. You tell yourself it's important to
be safe. Security comes first. It's a hard cruel world,
so you'd better play it safe now than be sorry later.
Fools rush in...

But nothing is more certain than that if you
walk down the centre of the road, you are going to
be hit by the traffic coming from both directions.

Playing it safe is the most dangerous
thing you can possibly do.

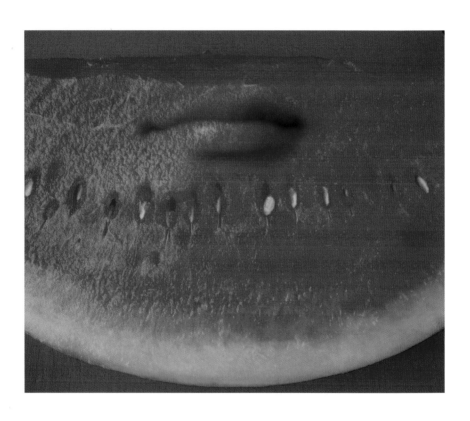

# 20 000 *words a day*
## *and most of them defamatory*

We speak to ourselves all the time.
Most days we direct around 20 000 words at
ourselves. Of these, nearly all are negative. We keep
feeding our minds with negative dialogue. How long
would you expect to keep a friend if you
did the same thing?

You *are* your own best friend. Start talking
to yourself nicely. Say kind things to yourself about
yourself. Believe. You'll be amazed at the difference
it makes to the person you know most
intimately and love the best.

*Superannuation is what we get paid for being bored for thirty years*

It seems to me we're obsessed with having things.

We put ourselves in debt for thirty years in order

to own a house. We work at thankless jobs we hate

for thirty years in order to have sufficient money to
retire with security and to die in absolute obscurity.

There is another way. The idea is to dream up
the things you want to do and make them happen.

Life is not about *having* things,
life is about *doing* things.

Doing things usually has a rewarding result.
You either make more money than you need without
being bored in the process, or you discover that you
don't really need all that fiscal security
to live happily ever after.

You also die smiling.

# *Putting a dream into action*

Nothing in the world can take the
place of persistence. Talent will not; nothing
is more common than unsuccessful men with talent.
Genius will not; unrewarded genius is almost
a proverb. Education will not; the world is full of
educated derelicts. Persistence and determination
alone are omnipotent. The slogan 'Press on'
has solved and always will solve the
problems of the human race.

*– Calvin Coolidge*

*I*t is as well to listen to someone with your eyes
as with your ears.

*A* gut feeling added to pure logic

is more powerful than logic used

all on its own.

$\mathcal{M}$an's greatest inheritance is the gift of speech.

The gift of words is the gift of imagination.

$\mathcal{W}$hile possibilities are horizons
without limit, we tend to create
our own fences.

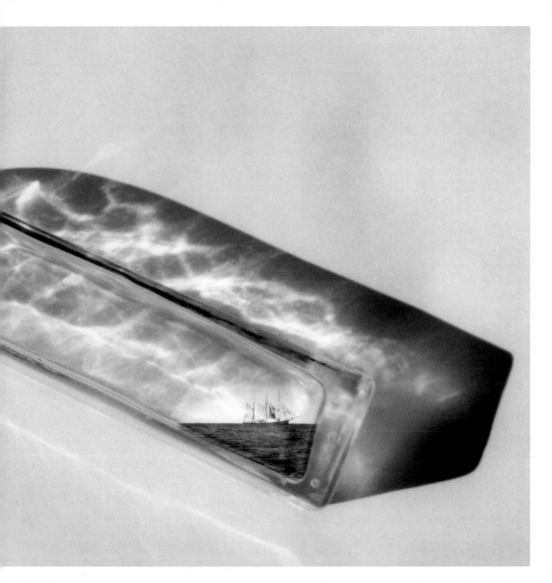

*U*nfortunately people generally see little benefit

in giving you the benefit of the doubt.

*I*f you tell yourself something can't
be done, you are creating an opportunity
for someone else to do it.

*W*hen we procrastinate we place the
art of living on standby.

*F*ailing to try is far worse than trying and failing.

*C*elebrity is no more than the first step

away from anonymity.

$W$hy is it that the happiest kids appear
to have fewer things?

*T*he mental abuse of a child is the equivalent of spraying agent orange on virgin jungle.

*B*efore you enter an argument,
ask yourself whether either outcome
is important to you.

the implacable tel
on th                              convinced that he
inhabit                            had broken down
m anothe      walls and           er, facing t
m the p        ke    in           s in t
a be    y I AM YOU
of a w        am dust particles
ng wom        I am the round sun
ore the
quatting     To the bits of dust I s
atched the    to the sun, *Keep movin*
e Pythia's
hall of the   I am morning mist,
vas a small   nd the breathing of ev
onsult the o  am wind in the top of
prophesied    nd surf on the cliff.
red to the
al stone wrap  Mast, rudder, helmsma
f th          I am also the coral reef
              ould hav
              accepted   otherwise I
              th the message. If anyth
              he responsibility.'
sterity. Not       d to detain the planet an
things under   planet would not sta
not wrong. It is   Southern Gate of
perience.      announced the
    It is the choi  y, I hereby procla    H
some little thing   rank is a high or
happy is to dec     nse.' Monkey gav
as your real self   mperor profusely      to
                    re ordered to b
    Q: Since there is   the Peach       and
pression of love of    e and Quiet      never.
M: Live your life int   Officers w    (turnin
        in mind.                  d Emm
                  re alre          d Heave
                  are       sat down, wait
                           mower.
                  riet, who was s
                  from her, did
                  speak, it was i
                  uld not have thou
                  ve misu    tood
                  but c     ring
                  hou      ha

$\mathcal{Y}$ou'll never know until you give it a go.

*– Anon*

*M*aking excuses usually denotes incompetence,

bad manners or self-pity.

thanks 4 yr help with hotels & contaᵗ

$S$ending an e-mail is not a thank-you note,

it is simply an electronic chore completed.

*J*ust because we are human doesn't mean
we need to behave like animals.

*W*hen we earn respect it is given freely;
when we demand it, it is given only
if we carry a big stick.

*A* sharp and painful truth is not always better than a soft word of comfort.

*W*e earn a reputation inch by inch,
but when it's gone, we lose it by miles.

*R*emember, when you chop down the tall poppies only the weeds remain.

*F*eeling sorry for yourself is the ultimate
self-indulgence; being happy in yourself
is the ultimate fulfilment.

*A* sharp tongue usually cuts before it thinks.

*If* you are too proud to say you're sorry

then you're too immature to be trusted to love.

*L*ife is too short to iron tea towels.

VIKING

Published by the Penguin Group
Penguin Group (Australia)
250 Camberwell Road, Camberwell, Victoria 3124, Australia
(a division of Pearson Australia Group Pty Ltd)
Penguin Group (USA) Inc.
375 Hudson Street, New York, New York 10014, USA
Penguin Group (Canada)
90 Eglinton Avenue East, Suite 700, Toronto, Canada ON M4P 2Y3
(a division of Pearson Penguin Canada Inc.)
Penguin Books Ltd
80 Strand, London WC2R 0RL England
Penguin Ireland
25 St Stephen's Green, Dublin 2, Ireland
(a division of Penguin Books Ltd)
Penguin Books India Pvt Ltd
11 Community Centre, Panchsheel Park, New Delhi – 110 017, India
Penguin Group (NZ)
67 Apollo Drive, Rosedale, North Shore 0632, New Zealand
(a division of Pearson New Zealand Ltd)
Penguin Books (South Africa) (Pty) Ltd
24 Sturdee Avenue, Rosebank, Johannesburg 2196, South Africa

Penguin Books Ltd, Registered Offices: 80 Strand, London, WC2R 0RL, England

First published 1994 by William Heinemann Australia
Reprinted 1994, 1996, 1998
First published by Penguin Books Australia Ltd, 1998
This revised edition published by Penguin Group (Australia), 2007

10 9 8 7 6 5 4 3 2 1

Design by Elizabeth Dias © Penguin Group (Australia)
Cover photograph and internal illustrations by Anie Williams
Typeset in 11/20pt Cochin Medium
Printed in China by 1010 Printing International Limited.

National Library of Australia
Cataloguing-in-Publication data:

Courtenay, Bryce, 1933- .
A recipe for dreaming.

ISBN 9780670028689.

1. Self-actualization (Psychology). 2. Optimism. I. Title.

158.1